Redefining Me!

Living & Loving the REAL YOU!

Dr. Amichia Jones

Address inquiries to
Jones Ministries International
P.O.Box 8092
Fayetteville, NC 28311
www.jonesministries.org

First Edition

Printed in the U.S.A.
Copyright © 2015Dr. Amichia Jones
All rights reserved.

ISBN-13: 978-0692552919

ISBN-10: 069255291X

Library of Congress Control Number:

All scripture quoted from The Authorized King James Version of the Bible
(Unless otherwise noted)

CONTENTS

INTRODUCTION

For the LORD will have mercy on Jacob, and will yet choose Israel, and set them in their own land: and the strangers shall be joined with them, and they shall cleave to the house of Jacob.

2 And the people shall take them, and bring them to their place: and the house of Israel shall possess them in the land of the LORD for servants and handmaids: and they shall take them captives, whose captives they were; and they shall rule over their oppressors.

3 And it shall come to pass in the day that the LORD shall give thee rest from thy sorrow, and from thy fear, and from the hard bondage wherein thou wast made to serve...Isaiah 14:1-3

God's greatest invention on the earth is mankind! We read in Genesis of how he carefully prepared and furnished the earth. I believe he dedicated the time and attention to it because he had special plans. Those plans have a lot to do with you and me. He want to give us everything that pertains to life and godliness. This life is filled with you pursuing and achieving your goals all while acquiring the enjoyment, fulfillment, and fellowship in Him.

Unfortunately, there are circumstances that arise in our lives which endeavor to limit or halt those plans. That is why it is imperative that we allow the God-like nature to surface from within us and overcome every negative obstacle. It is the will of God for you to have life and have it more abundantly! This means being free from past oppressive experiences, to include people that once blocked you.

God has your best interest at heart and will not stop at any cause from allowing you to receive all the promises he has for your life! The key to it is that you must do your part in not cowering down to the enemy! I look forward to seeing you win and live victoriously as the person God has originally designed you to be!

1
THE TASKMASTER

In the book of Exodus, we are introduced to 2
different people; the Israelites and the Egyptian
Pharaoh. The Israelites were Hebrew
descendents of Jacob whose ultimate fate was to
be released from oppression and pursue their
new life in Canaan as God's chosen people.

However, due to their massive growth in
numbers, fear and intimidation arose amongst
the Egyptians. The Egyptians encouraged

Pharaoh to shut down the Israelites and remove all hope and belief that what God had promised them would come to pass. The Egyptians took measures to suppress them, impede their growth, and keep them poor, eventually making them slaves. Taskmasters were placed over them to not only burden them, but to afflict them severely. This was the Taskmaster's strategy: (1.) to break their spirits, and rob them of everything in them that was honorable and generous. (2.) to ruin their health and shorten their days, and so diminish their numbers (3.) to discourage them from marrying since their children would be born to slavery. (4.) to oblige them to desert the Hebrews, and incorporate themselves with the Egyptians; thus hoping to cut off the name of Israel, that it might be no more in remembrance. Does any of this sound familiar to you? If so, I want to encourage you to keep reading this booklet. By the time you are done, you will be an entirely different person! In fact, you will no longer be oppressed or held bondage by any force of darkness. Perhaps you are dealing with a Taskmaster in this season of your life. His desire is to place fear and terror on you and make you believe that what God has promised you about yourself, your children, family, job, health, finances, etc... will not happen. Guess what my friend? God is not a god that should lie and He is watching over His word to perform it.

 His word shall not return back to him unaccomplished, it is going to be fulfilled! What or who is the Taskmaster that is stopping you? Is it people (family, friends, unhealthy relationships we create); could it be memories of tragic events that have caused you to be unforgiving; is it dealing with emotional, mental, alcoholic, or physical strongholds; is it disbelief in yourself because you have consistently compared/measured yourself to other people; or maybe you have discounted yourself because of your educational background and a lack of skills and training.

The bottom line is this: at some point in time, you agreed with a lie! You allowed someone or the circumstances you're facing to tell you that you could only accomplish so much, possess very little, and therefore an agreement with an untrue opinion was made.

As a result, you neglect to discover for yourself the potential that's locked within. When you fail to learn from God about who you are and what He has given you it is at this point you seek validation and approval from man. You open a door for people to define you based on their perception. Then, you exhibit the spirits of low self esteem, inferiority, and intimidation all because you agreed with a lie**!**

Every time the Israelites got stronger, the Taskmaster would throw them a blow. Have you ever been in a situation where you make the choice to improve your life and it seems as just as you start making progress, the enemy would all of a sudden attack you? You get a little bit further and you're attacked again? It's not just the attack that matters, but it's about your progress. He is after your progress. This is how you know that you are closer to your destiny.

Otherwise, there would be no pharaoh. No pharaoh, no purpose! He only goes after those with purpose!

I am reminded of the account of Jesus and the disciples preparing to "go to the other side" of the Sea of Galilee (Mark 4). Here they are, all gathered and ready to leave their current location to pursue another destination. The story opens with Jesus saying "Let". This implies the message that he is commanding the departure. This is powerful because if you are ever going to redefine who you are and change your current lifestyle, it requires that you COMMAND it! Yes, absolutely yes.

On their way, they were met with a great storm. This storm was so powerful and strong that the waves had caused the ship to become full of water. The enemy is not going to just easily allow you to leave. In fact, he does not expect for you to leave or believe that you have the willpower to leave. When you command something, it speaks to the authority and right that you have. It speaks to the fact that there is a demand rising up from within you that announces and commands for every obstacle and stronghold in your life to relinquish its power!

This storm responded to Jesus' command as forceful opposition. This force was after Jesus'

intentions of making forward progression.
There will be forces of opposition that you will
be confronted with that are in direct
contradiction to your decision to progress
forward. In fact, this storm had presented itself
in such a powerful way because Jesus was not
only changing the course of his journey, but the
course of others! The other little ships
mentioned in Mark 4 speaks of those who
wanted to progress ahead as well! So, just know
that your decision to redefine your life, to get
out and live free, has the propensity to snatch
others out of the same pit of oppression! And
you thought that you were in this state by
yourself!?!?

Jesus handled the opposition by speaking as
one of authority, staying in faith and fully
believing that the destination that he had set
out to reach would come to pass! So my friend,
I want to encourage you to stay in faith and do

not overreact with fear. Most importantly, remain fully convinced that you will begin again!

Your weapons to fight the enemy are not based on your emotions and other natural means. No, no, no. You must remain in the spirit of Christ and cause the strength and the power of God to rise up from within you and boldly profess your freedom! God has not given you fear or timidity, He has given you power, love and a sound mind!

 I want to encourage you to grab hold of revelation knowledge! Here it is: you are the righteousness of God and He has given you power to get wealth; you are the head and not the tail; you are a lender to many nations and not a borrower. God has given you power to tread over serpents and scorpions; no evil shall befall you and regardless of the infirmity you may be experiencing in your body, no plague can come nigh your dwelling because you belong to God!

According to the Taskmaster, you are not supposed to have vision. And somehow, God has given you a glimpse into your future. You're starting to break barriers and push through opposition and he doesn't like that. Why? You are supposed to stay complacent. You are supposed to accept your life the way it is! But my friend, God has told us not to look at the things that are seen, but look at what is not seen. In other words take your eyes off of your situation(s) and what you are going through. The Taskmaster and everything about you is only temporary and about to change! Glory to God! Have your mind made up TODAY that you are pressing toward the mark of deliverance and a new life of freedom in Christ. God says to "bind the strongman and spoil his house!" In another scripture, we are encouraged to bind the Word of God as tables on our heart. The word "bind" means to tie up or fasten around or fix in place. When someone or something has been bound, movement has become restricted and it is very unlikely that it will loosen (on its own).

See what God has to say about you! In Him there are no limits or boundaries! You can achieve all that you desire to achieve! You can do all things through Him because it is from Him you draw strength. It doesn't matter what other people have done or what you may or may not have accomplished. Pull out of your potential from the depths of your most inner self and just believe! There is a Canaan awaiting your arrival! Lasso your pharaoh! He is a defeated foe, not you! Every yoke of bondage, self defeat, discouragement, emotional hurt, etc…has been destroyed because of the anointing!

2
LET ME GO

Think about a time where you were placed in a situation that required you to demonstrate expressing a position you strongly believed in? How adamant were you? How secure are you in your position of liberty when it comes to being free from old mindsets, stagnation, memory of disappointments and troubled pasts, sicknesses and diseases and plaguing circumstances of today?

Your freedom is contingent upon how much

you are willing to fight for it!So, you must determine how badly you desire it. Let's look at it like this- How much value or worth have you placed on your brand new start? You have to evaluate this because as discussed earlier, the taskmaster is not willing to let you go. Therefore, tighten up your boot straps, get your boxing gloves on and as they say in the world of boxing, "Let's get ready to rumble!!!!!!!"

The widow woman and the unjust judge

18 1-3 Jesus told them a story showing that it was necessary for them to pray consistently and never quit. He said, "There was once a judge in some city who never gave God a thought and cared nothing for people. A widow in that city kept after him: 'My rights are being violated. Protect me!'

4-5 "He never gave her the time of day. But after this went on and on he said to himself, 'I care nothing what God thinks, even less what people think. But because this widow won't quit badgering me, I'd better do something and see that she gets justice— otherwise I'm going to end up beaten black-and- blue by her pounding.'"

6-8 Then the Master said, "Do you hear what that judge, corrupt as he is, is saying? So what makes you think God won't step in and work justice for his chosen people, who continue to cry out for help? Won't he stick up for them? I assure you, he will. He will not drag his feet. But how much of that kind of persistent faith will the Son of Man find on the earth when he returns? Luke 18:1-8 MSG

I think that this is a very good scenario in the Bible that you and I can perhaps relate to. This is the story of a widow woman who went before the courts to seek vengeance upon someone who had inflicted harm to her. Although we are not told of what her opponent had done, we do know that they are considered an enemy. Despite the judge's stern lack of empathy, he granted her what she desired and that was vengeance! I am certain that she walked out of that court room as an entirely different woman — A liberated, restored, and most important...a **FAVORED** woman! Isn't that powerful? Glory to God!

Every day, since the onset of her being scrutinized, receiving evil taunts, all while wearing looks of exhaustion, weariness, and frustration sure enough presented a never-ending battle for her. But not anymore! The courts saw fit to overturn the opponent's argument. How was it possible that this woman was able to win her case? How was it possible that she was able to get this judge, who Jesus had even said was corrupt and had no regard (care for either him or her) to have a change of heart? One word — PERSISTENCE!

Persistence calls for a person to not quit, but continually remain steadfast or firm in their position. It also describes someone as being tenacious. Are you a person of tenacity? Colossians 2:7 tells us that we are to be *"Rooted and built up in him, and stablished in the faith, as ye have been taught, abounding therein with thanksgiving."*

What is this saying? Jesus is telling us that not for any moment should we be willing to waver in what we want. Why? As long as you are connected to him, feeding yourself with the Word of God, it will strengthen and make you unbreakable in your mind and spirit. Your faith will come out of you as a strong force, shielding you. The taskmaster, or oppressor, may be telling you that it is not going to release your finances, health, family, job, etc... but do not allow what is said to pull you apart or break you down. You will not break under pressure! I rebuke every spirit of agony that has been launched against your will power IN JESUS' NAME! I speak that you will become stubborn in the spirit---in every good sense of the word--- unbreakable, not giving in, and resistant to the forces of darkness!

This is a great moment right here for you to do as the latter part of Colossians 2:7 reads and that is thank God! Yes, right now!! Thank him in advance for what is just around the corner. Baal Perazim himself…that is, THE GOD OF MASTER BREAKTHROUGH is on the way and He is bringing his army to fight. Victory has already been declared on your behalf.

Refuse to take no for an answer! You have to leave the earth realm and take your case to the spirit realm which is, the Government of God! The Government of God is the highest authority, the supreme authority, and never loses a case. When you take your matters before

"The Judge Almighty", it means that you are letting the spiritual system of Heaven represent you. You realize that what is at hand is bigger than you and therefore requires a bigger, more powerful force. Jesus cancels every guilty verdict and reminds the enemy of the written Word -No weapon that has been formed against you shall prosper! The enemy has no choice but to render you what is just because when God speaks, that is the final say! He must submit to the authority and commands of God! Matthew 16:19 tells us that what you bind on earth is bound in Heaven. In other words, whatever is taking place in the earth, must resemble what is going on in the heavenlies. They must be in sync with one another, in fact, earth must come into sync with heaven. This is the only way and anything that is contrary or out of alignment with the Lord will be dealt with accordingly.

The widow woman of Luke 18 made it a point to show up in the courtroom every day. She determined within herself to be visible. Do you realize that your presence speaks volumes? The enemy is counting on you not showing up. In fact, he desires that you remain absent and uninvolved in the activities in the course of your life. When you make your presence known, it sends a warning to the kingdom of darkness. An announcement has gone forth that this time, you mean business! Yes, this time is unlike the times of past. You have allowed the Lord to build you up in your most holy faith; you have been meditating and confessing the Word of God; and your confidence in Him tells you that you are invincible. So, this time you will fight and you will win! You are going to have to be relentless in attaining victory, a new life, or even change.

"And give him no rest, till he establish, and till he make Jerusalem a praise in the earth". Isaiah 62:7 KJV

When you become relentless, you have made up in your mind that you will not let up until you get what you want. Relentless people, I believe, have seen something. God allows them to receive a glimpse of what their life is like on the other side of bondage. They taste victory and therefore, resolve within themselves to satisfy that strong appetite.

In turn, they embrace what God has shown them and develop willpower to make it happen. Jacob (Genesis 28:12-15) had a dream of a ladder with angels going up and down it. God showed him that he had access to something far greater than anything on the earth. He had access to the heavens. Scripture tells us in Deuteronomy 28 that *"The LORD shall open unto thee his good treasure, the heaven to give the rain*

21

unto thy land in his season, and to bless all the work of thine hand..."

Listen my friend, you are just like Jacob! You have access to an open heaven. The Lord is letting you know that you have a supernatural support system. The entire host of Heaven has been assigned to fully, I mean fully, back you. The Angels are contending for you as you contend (fight) for the faith. Glory to God! It is comforting to know that you and I have the support of our Father.

3
I WILL LET YOU GO BUT…

Pharoah told Moses that he would permit him
and the Israelites to leave Egypt, but it was
based on a particular criterion. The agreement
would be that the Israelites would remain
within viewing distance. What Pharaoh was
saying was this, "I am willing to release you as
long as I can see you!" Pharoah, like many
people today, was not completely ready to
surrender control over the Israelites. And as
long as they remained within reachable
distance, he would still have the ability to place

restrictions upon them. I would like to offer a challenge to you. DARE to remove the controlling and manipulative strings from off of you! For quite some time, you have lived according to someone else's standards and have allowed them to define who you are, what you like or dislike, how you wear your hair, where you live and the like thereof. You cannot I repeat, cannot afford to negotiate with the enemy.

At one time or another, did you find yourself asking, "How did I get here?" Well, quite simply, when we abandon the will to please God and live according to his standards or right way of living we become people pleasers. We work hard at gaining their approval and acceptance, not realizing that we are compromising a life of freedom, happiness, and well-being.

It is for freedom that Christ has set us free. Stand firm, then, and do not let yourselves be burdened again by a yoke of slavery. Gal. 5:1

You have been set free! It was already provided for you by the finished works of the cross. So, what exactly am I saying? I am saying that you are ALREADY free from other people's limitations, boundaries, opinions and ideas! So now it is time to REDISCOVER and REDEFINE YOU! Tell Pharaoh to LET YOU GO!

The Israelites eventually removed themselves as far away from Egypt and soon settled in the wilderness. However, they received instructions from the Lord in Joshua Chapter 1, that it was now time to keep going and cross over to the other side of the Jordan. He is giving those same instructions to you... bring a closure to grave and desert conditions in your life!

The wilderness was never meant to become a permanent place dwelling place for you. It is to only serve as a passageway for you to strip off and shed old mindsets, behaviors and relationships. The Israelites had made some forward progress in their journey, but due to their inability to strip off their old ways and slave-like mentality, they only moved in circles.

When you refuse to conform to the wonderful life in Christ that eagerly awaits you, your life will only keep you going in circles. Instead of making progress, you will only find yourself accomplishing very little (at the hands of Pharoah) and remain stuck. Things will not fall in place and your life will utterly revert to a state of turmoil and confusion.

My friend, I have exciting news for you! Your days of living in confusion and frustration have come to an end! There are promises and blessings that await your arrival in Canaan and in order for you to obtain them, you must crossover! Allow the VICTORIOUS nature in you to RISE UP and start marching now!

Let this mind be in you, which was also in Christ Jesus. Phil 2:5

God told the Israelites on several occasions to "be strong and of good courage". Why would He continuously tell them that? He knew that somewhere in their minds there was corrupt thinking. Corrupt thinking produces negative outcomes and will prevent you from overtaking the enemy. Where the enemy planted words of inferiority, past failures, low self esteem, and discouragement, God uproots and replaces them with words of empowerment. These words build your faith and create new images in your heart. Faith comes by hearing the Word of God. As long as you are hearing God's word on a consistent basis, negative images will be torn down. It won't be too far long where you will begin thinking, believing, seeing and carrying yourself as an overcomer!

Start preparing for the mental shifting. This means that as Christ transforms you into a newer you, you will take on his mind! Your new mind now causes you to daily think about things that are lovely, honest, pure and gives you a mind of life and peace. Rather than having a subservient mindset, nature and attitude, you will set your affections on things above, looking outwardly and in anticipation of good things to come! You are going to be done away with feeling condemned, having ill and distorted views and speaking foolishly about yourself. Why? Because, you are the righteousness of God through faith in Christ Jesus! Glory! You deserve all that He has for you. Therefore, stop thinking that you do not have enough money to buy your home, take that dream vacation, or attend college. Refrain from believing that you lack the skill and ability to land that promotion or start your business. You are not from the Egyptian system of barely making it or just getting by. NO!

Your Father has left you loaded and you are from a Kingdom of wealth, abundance, and overflow. You are a child of the Most High, so let the Kingdom of Heaven be manifested in your life, on your job, in your family, in your finances, etc. Regardless of how much the enemy will try to fight and go against what you are pursuing, continue to tell yourself that you can go, have and do all things because the greater one is within you!

4

THE WINNER WITHIN

God never creates anything to only just exist!
Why? Well, He would not receive any glory or
praise from it. Every person, place or thing that
has been created has significant purpose. This
applies to you as well, my friend! Your life was
created with a purpose and serves far more of a
meaning than what or where you are right now.
Negative things that happen in life are only
meant to attack our drive and reason to live. In
those cases, people accept negative outcomes
as their final story. They become angry at God

and the world. They stop pursuing their dreams, lose ambition and eventually drawback and shut down. You ABSOLUTELY CANNOT be one of them!

There is a winner within you! I highly encourage you that now is the best time for you to begin at life again. You are one moment away from your life becoming better. Your moment starts with a decision and you must decide immediately to change.

Let's look at John 5:1-9:

"1After this there was a feast of the Jews; and Jesus went up to Jerusalem. 2Now there is at Jerusalem by the sheep market a pool, which is called in the Hebrew tongue Bethesda, having five porches. 3In these lay a great multitude of impotent folk, or blind, halt, withered, waiting for the moving of the water. 4For an angel went down at a certain season into the pool, and troubled the water: whosoever then first after the troubling of the water stepped in was made whole of whatsoever disease he had. 5And a certain man was there, which had an

infirmity thirty and eight years. ⁶When Jesus saw him lie, and knew that he had been now a long time in that case, he saith unto him, Wilt thou be made whole? ⁷The impotent man answered him, Sir, I have no man, when the water is troubled, to put me into the pool: but while I am coming, another steppeth down before me. ⁸Jesus saith unto him, Rise, take up thy bed and walk. ⁹And immediately the man was made whole, and took up his bed, and walked: and on the same day was the sabbath.

This story discusses a man lying at the Pool of Bethesda. We are told that people who suffered from various forms of sicknesses gathered there. They were waiting for an opportunity to be healed.

I find it very interesting how John points out to us that this man had been in his *dis*eased condition for quite some time. Jesus approached the gentleman and asked him a very simple question… "Do you want to become well?"

This question is the most important question that one could ever be asked. It reveals the gateway to improvement… breakthrough…victory…change!

Hallelujah!

It puts the intended person in a position of closing the doors of every sorrowful, unpleasant or bad memory encountered.

So, Jesus is posing that same question to you today! Do you want to improve your life? Are you really earnest in your intentions and desires for a brand new start? Now, before you answer that question, let me warn you. Jesus is not interested in any of your excuses, Therefore, you must reframe from giving any. He is not concerned about the past events of your life or the people involved. That information is completely irrelevant and not useful for where you are headed.

The man lying at the pool immediately began making excuses before he gave him a yes. Your change requires an immediate YES. That "yes" denotes a definitive response. When you are tired of shifting the responsibility on others, you will change. There are two steps however, that I would like to point out as you start to change. The first step involves decision making, followed by the assuming of responsibility.

Decision making involves you being given a choice. Responsibility is where you take charge of the choice made. So determine whether or not you want things to improve or remain the same. When it comes to decision making, you must access yourself to determine if you are capable of handling everything that comes with the choice you make.

Acknowledge any convictions. Convictions come to awaken us to our neglect. Rather than internalizing and becoming depressed, just repent.

Develop a can do attitude. Set small goals and give yourself credit for what you currently can do to improve!

Keep the commitment you've made. Once you develop steadfastness and determination, you are well on your way to winning.

Pray. Develop a prayer life that works for you. There is nothing like communicating with the Lord and allowing His spirit to guide you along your mass exodus.

Rise Up! If there is an urge of readiness inside of you, then allow it to be followed up by a performance. Consistent execution over a period of time becomes a lifestyle. This new lifestyle you will develop will be a result of your commitment and honesty.

Be patient. The Lord will perfect those things that you are confronted with along the way. As you move forward, obstacles will try to halt you and bring error...just get back up and remain diligent!

Please hear my heart for you when you read this next statement. Cooperate with God when He says, "You can do this!" When you do so, a conquering spirit is created. This force arises from within you and defeats every enemy of fear, stagnation, discouragement, intimidation and inferiority.

Again, I hear the Lord saying the word "**RELENTLESS**". Praise God! That means that whatever taskmaster tries to rear its ugly head at you will not break your spirit. You will be unyielding and will not compromise. Persevere beyond your present day in order to get to the freedom that awaits you. I would like to challenge you to get thirsty for it! Isaiah 44:3 proclaims,

 "For I will pour water upon him that is thirsty, and floods upon the dry ground: I will pour my spirit upon thy seed, and my blessing upon thine offspring."

You have a promise of remedy for every difficulty. Refreshing waters are coming into your life for every parched and quenched area. It is up to you to heed to the call of your spirit to be revitalized, refreshed, and empowered.

5

REINVENT YOURSELF

The most important question that you must ask
yourself is, "Who does God say that I am?"
Why, you might ask? Well, that is the most
important piece of information of which really
matters.

Friends and family will define you based on
commonalities and these result in you living a
limited and restricted life. However, when the
Lord defines your life, He bases it on love,
uniqueness, life, power a most importantly His

IMAGE!

When you consider the meaning of the word reinvent, it is defined as making something over in a different form. It also means to make major changes or improvement. The bottom line is this-- by the time you have escaped the life that you were familiar with and God makes you over, you are going to be re-presented as an entirely different person!

You will no longer be the person that people have perhaps manipulated, ran over, or used. You will be a new person that is full of joy, laughter, and adventure! I am soo excited for you! For far too long, people and past relationships have placed you in a sealed box. You laughed when they told you to laugh; you were acknowledged when they felt that you should be acknowledged; and maybe, just maybe, you were the one who did all of their errands. All of those things and not to mention the other busy work that you found yourself doing ended up leaving you exhausted, burnt out and no good for your own affairs. These remember, is what we stated at the beginning of the book—the Taskmaster's attempts at eradicating your identity.

Getting back to my original question—the reason that you must ask God about yourself is because He is the creator of everything! He is the one who gave you life into this world and of course, the new life that awaits you. If I may, let me bring you in on a little secret. The Lord placed every great and small detail about your personality, instincts, and how you think inside of you. He knows what makes you cry, laugh, and yes even volatile. He knows how to get you moving and what things will distract and take you off focus! Let's just say that if there is anything that you need to know about yourself, consult the manufacturer! There sits in Heaven, with your name attached, is a little instruction manual that has information about your life, responses to life, and things that you have not even begun to tap into yet.

"But as it is written, Eye hath not seen, nor ear heard, neither have entered into the heart of man, the things which God hath prepared for them that love him." I Cor. 2:9

I am not sure of if you have had the time to think about this, but the Lord has great and exciting plans for you! Isn't that wonderful to know? He is looking forward to you taking that initial step into discovering all the promises that are in Him. According to Jeremiah 29: 11, He has plans to prosper you and give you the future that you hope for. This means, He plans on getting involved in every intricate decision and process of your life. You know, the interesting thing about that is that He was there with you the entire time! And certainly my friend, the Lord does not plan on abandoning you---ever. As I often tell people, he has your best interest at heart.

Spiritual Makeover

I am reminded of an old television show that was once popular in the US, named *Extreme Makeover: Home Edition.* This show highlighted selected families who were given an opportunity of having their home completely renovated. The team of home interior designers and all skilled laborers involved in the house project would have just seven days to complete the work. This demolition project involved reconstructing an entirely new house - every single room, plus the exterior and landscaping, looking nothing like its former design.

Wow! That's a word right there. You're getting ready to experience a demolishing of old memories, corrupt thinking, and habits that you and everyone that knew you were familiar with.

And may I just add this tidbit of information? This also serves as a wonderful opportunity for you to perhaps, indulge in what I like to say, "pampering and loving me" sessions. I'm not talking about hair and nail salon visits, although that is just as important! What I am referring to is making your overall health and well-being a number one priority.

Now that you have begun to work on your inner self, it is time to let it show forth outwardly! Absolutely! Your well being flows inside out as a reflection of your inward spirit. You should explore ideas of receiving medical aesthetic treatments, such as facials and massages. And if you are really daring and ready, why not consider cosmetic surgery! What!???! It is not taboo and should not be viewed (in my opinion) as such. More and more people are seeking cosmetic treatments to help them maintain their physical appearance, heal from an abusive past, and improve their confidence.

I have witnessed accounts of people who have received such services. Their overall response have all been the same, feeling "revitalized and refreshed". As you embrace your new lifestyle and adopt a healthier diet, you will become more proactive in looking after your temple.

Beloved, I wish above all things that thou mayest prosper and be in health, even as thy soul prospereth. 3 John 2

As you become more confident in the REAL you, coupled with a good health status, it appears as evidence in the workplace, your social situations and relationships, and you will be more empowered and able to set new and accomplish goals. So, there we have it! This demolition project is necessary and can no longer be put off for where you are headed. What you did and how you carried out your life in Egypt will not be of any use (or value) when you reach Canaan! Besides, you do not want to take any of those behaviors with you.

> *"Behold, I will do a new thing; now it shall spring forth; shall ye not know it?"Isa. 43:19*

The Lord is getting ready to do a new thing in you! As He tells us in his word, his Spirit is going to come upon you. When? Well, at the moment you surrender and begin your exodus from bondage. For every distasteful episode, He is smearing you in the oil of joy. For every hurtful, disappointing, embarrassing and

Redefining Me!

challenging event in your life, there will be an emptying taking place. When you relinquish the weight of carrying it all, you shall remember them no more. For your shame, including any emotional damages that you have received, you shall have abundant recompense.

Get ready for a brand new identity! God has called you by a brand new name. He is calling you by the name He originally gave you, not the name the Taskmaster gave you. When Daniel and his four friends were taken into captivity by King Nebuchadnezzar, their names were changed. In fact, their names were changed to reflect the idolatrous practices and lifestyle of that time. This is very important because Daniel and his friends' names were originally Hebrew and therefore had meaning.

So what am I saying? I am telling you that your name has meaning and purpose. Your name

45

identifies your significance in this world. You were not brought here to be held under bondage. No! Your purpose is far greater than that!

Start looking back into the things that you once enjoyed doing—hobbies, special interests, and so forth. I guarantee that they will lead to a clue or two of what you are supposed to be doing. Your new name will not be the name that everybody in the neighborhood addressed you as. Nor will it be the family nickname you inherited. Those names were not full of meaning and purpose. If anything, they only served as constant reminder to you of an unfruitful and regretful past. So, I would like to encourage you to embrace your new identity now! Embrace your passions and the things that give you joy. Start telling people "no" when you cannot commit to things that are of no benefit and interest to you. Will you be unsettled and uncomfortable at first? Sure, but the more you stand on your decision, the easier it will become. You have to remember that people were used to you giving in, at the drop of a dime at your expense.

What you must embrace is the concept of not responding the way that someone else would. This is how you send your "courtesy message" of change. People have now begun to observe whether or not and how long you are going to hold true to the new you. The moment you respond how they would expect you to, will support their notion that you really have not changed. It would relay a message of you still holding onto areas of insecurity and inferiority. God has created you as a superior, top ranking individual! There is nothing substandard about you. You can go and enjoy life! You can be the adventurous person you had dreamed of becoming. Make plans to go on vacation. The point I am trying to make is this---Shells of boredom and mundane feelings can plant seeds of fear and doubt and leave many people stuck where they are. That is not the case for you! Shout it out real loud "I shall not die, but live and declare the works of the Lord!" Yes, that is it. Claim your life back immediately! From this moment on, you can no longer suppress the inward cry. You must release it, let it go, and dance your way to Canaan.

Canaan is your new homeland. It is a land of provision, safety, and plush living. I suggest plush because anytime the Lord is involved in your life, he always does it BIG and BETTER and of course, ABUNDANTLY than what you could ever fathom. There is nothing in Canaan that speaks of mediocre living or barely enough. Joshua, Caleb, and the ten spies brought back the evidence of that land. What they discovered was that the land was full of the best of the best, the crème de la crème, that it would make anyone forget the former life of bondage (Num. 13: 23, 27). And that is exactly what the Lord intends for you. When you step out of the old and step into the new you, what is awaiting you is so big that it is going make you forget about the life you once lived! Glory to God! That makes me want to just step into the new along with you! But as much as I would love to, I can't and neither can anyone else! Well, the Lord does not want you to be dependent upon anyone to aid or come to your rescue. You must know that He is your ONLY source! Yes, it has been easy to look for others to be there for you. But those instances created false dependencies. Remember when I shared earlier with you that the Lord has always been there with you? Well, that is still true even in Canaan. He desires to have fellowship and share with you in this new place. He desires to be involved!

As you go forward, you are going to see just how much of a true friend and support system He is! Something else that you will discover is that your faith and assurance will grow. Each new step forward that you take will eradicate every feeling of low self worth, disbelief, and discouragement. Continue to shatter the box of limitations that once held you back.

As you begin your new journey, I would like to offer some suggestions that will help you.

Take a moment and find out what really defines you. You should focus on the areas that can positively change the course of your world. For some people, their focus is family. While for others, their defining focus is their career. Focusing on what defines you will inspire you to set new standards for yourself.

Cultivate new qualities that express your personality. Make a list of qualities that you would like to be known for. Some people enjoy being known as a sports enthusiast or a great cook. Others enjoy being known as a risk taker or being an adventurer. As you create your list, it will help reach your goals of living and loving the REAL YOU!

Create a vision board. Having a visual plan motivates you to keep going in times of frustration, anxiety, and unbelief. Seeing it every day serves as a constant reminder that everything you are working towards is possible!

Follow your passions and do what you love doing. What passions have you put off or forgotten about due to a lack of opportunity? Now is the time to get busy with them and do not say that you are too old to do it! Perhaps you are passionate about running a marathon, starting a non-profit organization, becoming a consultant, acting or changing your career. Whatever the passion, just know that you have been anointed for it! Instead of looking at those passions as something hard or impossible, look at it as an opportunity waiting to be seized! I just hear the Lord saying so softly, "Trust me!" It is so worth it! In fact, it is worth it all — all of the steps in life that you have taken to get to the place where you are now! Steps of wondering "what if", "I don't know if it will work" and even this one, "Help me!" Do you recall making any of those statements? Well if so, you have entered into the realm of total reliance and trust in the Lord. And this is the place where you are suppose to be! He will never misguide you. After all of the statements that you made then, look where you are now! You are still happy and free.

Yes, you made the right decision. Just keep walking by faith and do not take your eyes off of the Lord!

MINISTRY INFORMATION

Jones Ministries International (JMI) is designed to inspire and equip Christian leaders through the anointing of God with the tools to build Bible based churches and ministries that will impact the world.

The intent of JMI is to link faith- minded believers together, empowered to fulfill the great commission and transfer the end-time harvest into the Kingdom of God. JMI's purpose is:

1. To help empower JMI covenant partners in fulfilling the ministry and/or calling to which God has called them.

2. To provide an avenue for networking and fellowship among the JMI partnership.

3. To supply a vehicle through while JMI can share information and make available resources and training that will benefit JMI partners in their pursuit of excellence in ministry and Kingdom building.

4. To establish a board from the ministerial alliance members, for the purpose of licensing, ordination, and especially ministry accountability.

5. To provide Biblically-based teaching and various ministry resources to equip church leaders and ministries to reach increasing numbers of unchurched people.

The Global Teaching Network (GTN) provides individual and ministry specific trainings upon request. The A.I.M.S. Bible Institute and School of Ministry is one of many auspices under the GTN umbrella. Drs. Antonio & Amichia Jones serve as the President and Vice-President, respectively, of JMI's operations. They have been married for more than 12 years.

Please visit the website @ **www.jonesministries.org**

To contact Dr. Amichia Jones:

Jones Ministries International
P.O. BOX 8092
Fayetteville, NC 28311

Email: jonesministries4@gmail.com